W9-ARC-808

When I Am Afraid

When I Am Afraid

A STEP-BY-STEP GUIDE
AWAY FROM FEAR AND ANXIETY

Edward T. Welch

New
Growth
Press

www.newgrowthpress.com

New Growth Press, Greensboro, NC 27429
Copyright © 2010 by Edward T. Welch. All rights reserved.
Published 2010.

Unless noted otherwise, all Scripture quotations are from the New International Version, copyright © 1973, 1978, 1984 by International Bible Society. Used by permission of Zondervan. All rights reserved.

Cover Design: The DesignWorks Group,
Nate Salciccioli and Jeff Miller, www.designworksgroup.com

Typesetting: Lisa Parnell

ISBN-13: 978-1-935273-15-8
ISBN-10: 1-935273-15-9

Printed in Canada

17 16 15 14 13 12 11 10   1 2 3 4 5

To
*Covenant Life Church in Gaithersburg
and The Sovereign Grace churches*
for their kindness and generosity

Author's Note

This workbook is a complement to *Running Scared: Fear, Worry, and the God of Rest,* but it is not a chapter-by-chapter study guide for that book. It is intended to stand alone as a study guide for individuals and groups.

Contents

Getting Started

Fear is the perfect problem. No doubt, it can be paralyzing and painful. When it comes, your goal is to get rid of it immediately. By its very nature fear tells you to run rather than face whatever is causing it. The problem can be life-dominating. But it is ideal in this: God reserves his most persuasive, beautiful, and comforting words for fearful people. If you are familiar with fear, and we all are, get ready to hear something good.

You have heard the Psalm that begins, "The LORD is my shepherd" (Psalm 23:1). It is timeless and comforting, but it sounds good only if you are familiar with fear and anxiety.

"Never will I leave you; never will I forsake you" (Hebrews 13:5). It is God's most frequent and comforting promise. They are beautiful words, but you have to know about fear and anxiety for them to be God's words to you.

"Peace to you" (Galatians 1:3). It can sound like an ordinary, if old-fashioned, greeting; but if fear and anxiety are your companions, they are wonderful words, filled with hope.

So get your pen handy and get ready to listen to God's Word. Really listen. Because when you really listen, you can't help but respond. When you hear beautiful and comforting words that surpass anything you could imagine, you do something. You are moved into action. You tell other people. You believe. You are changed.

This study guide is designed to help you meditate on what God says to fearful and anxious people. It stretches over seven weeks. That way you will have more time to meditate on the Bible until fear and anxiety begin to yield ground to hope, peace, and rest. Spend twenty minutes or so each day reading and answering the questions. Replacing fear and anxiety with peace and rest is a lifelong task, but seven weeks, twenty minutes a day, can kick-start the process.

It unfolds this way. In the first two weeks you will identify fear and anxiety, listen to what it is really saying, and proceed to the story of how God provided miraculous food (manna) for his children. This story about manna will be your foundation for much that God will say to you about fear.

With basic tools in hand, in the following three weeks you will consider the three most common categories of fear: fear of not having enough money, fear of death, and fear of the opinions or violence of other people.

The last two weeks will reflect on how God makes promises of faithfulness to his people and swears that he will keep those promises. Psalm 46 will also be on the docket, with one application being that you are able to focus on today because you know that the Lord will be with you tomorrow.

When possible, go through this workbook with a friend or small group. God has determined that change typically occurs in the context of a community. There you can learn from others, put words onto your experience, glean from the Bible together, be prayed for, and pray for others. Isn't it like God to make the path of change enjoyable?

And what do you get at the end of your seven-week investment? Indomitable, warriorlike, nothing-can-intimidate-you courage—or maybe something a little more modest and better. While "nonstop freedom from fear and anxiety" might sound good at first, if that happened, difficult circumstances would never be a time to turn to your strong King. Instead, you would just trust in yourself, which is part of the problem and is the very last thing we would want.

What you are aiming for are better goals:

- You want to hone your spiritual instincts so that you turn to Jesus when you are anxious, rather than trusting in your ability to solve or deny problems.

- You want to know what Jesus says because when you turn to him in this way his words go deep.
- You want to be less fearful and anxious and more content and hopeful.
- You want to be more confident that God's communication to you in the Bible speaks meaningfully to *all* the struggles of life.

That, my friend, is what awaits you.

Week 1

Fear and Anxiety Speak Out

In the first week, you are going to locate fear and anxiety and listen to them. Of course, because they find *you,* the search is easy. But the more you see them, the more you will benefit from God's words to fearful and anxious people.

To be human is to be afraid.

We are small; the world is big. Though we make plans, follow through on decisions, and feel like we have some say-so, we can't control even the most trivial events. Amass enough money to keep creditors at bay, then death comes knocking at your door. Lock the door to secure all your belongings, then rust and decay steal your fortune from within.

Neither is there any consolation in being poor. It's true that the less you have the less there is to lose, and if you are poor you may be less vulnerable to thievery, but you may still worry about being out on the street and finding your next meal. Having material possessions can make you feel as though a buffer is between you and . . . whatever is out there that is so creepy.

Feeling better now? Don't worry, the story ends well.

FIND YOUR FEARS

The first step toward overcoming your fears is to locate them—and to locate a lot of them. The attractiveness of God's words to you depends on it. If you can't see your fears and worries, then God's words of comfort won't go deep.

So, just for the sake of this exercise, go ahead and assume that you are absolutely riddled with fears. Find one, and you will find dozens more. Fear, anxieties, and worries are pack animals. They always travel in groups.

⇨ What fears and worries can you locate immediately?

⇨ What fears do you have regarding those people you love?

⇨ Fears and worries arise when we could lose something important to us—
something we love. What are you afraid you could lose?

⇨ What fears do you have about your own death and possible physical disability?

⇨Any specific fears? If your specific fear is not listed here, add it to the bottom row.

The Dark	Blood	Needles
Airplanes	Confinement	Animals
Water	Germs	Heights
Disease	Clowns	Crowds

Whatever fears you have, you can be sure you are not alone. Just tell a few people you are beginning a study about fear, anxiety, and worry. Ask them for their thoughts. What fears do they have? How do they deal with them? Go ahead; try it.

Your conversation will accomplish two things. First, it will confirm that you are not crazy. Your seemingly very normal neighbors can probably top your fears. Second, your conversation will turn you outward. One of the ways of wisdom is to look outside of ourselves and care about the interests of others.

LISTEN TO YOUR FEARS

Your emotions are a kind of language. Anger, embarrassment, happiness, grief, guilt—they all say something. For example, anger says, "It's your fault." Listen more carefully and it says, "I am authorized to stand in judgment of you."

Fear, too, is saying something, and you would be wise to listen. It says, "Run for the hills," and "Avoid, deny, pretend it's not going to happen." Anything else?

⇨What might your fears and anxieties be truly saying?

Fear and anxiety make a prediction. One of their messages is clear. Fear and anxiety both live in the future. They say, "There is a future threat to something I love." We fancy ourselves as prophets, and we keep trusting in our predictions even though they don't come to pass. Fear and worry are prophecies. Check out the fears you listed, and see if this fits.

⇨What prediction is your fear making?

Fear and worry say something about our relationship with God. Now let's go one more step. When we listen to fear and worry, we can usually notice that we are predicting the worst, and we can often detect the connection with things or people we love. But it is more difficult to hear what our fears are saying about our relationship with God.

So listen even more carefully because fears and worries have *everything* to do with him.

You can see how God is connected to everything when a little child keeps asking "why" questions. Start anywhere: "Why do I have a nose?" "Why do I have to go to bed?" "Why do I have to eat peas?" "Why is the sky blue?" Before the fifth why, your answer has probably become, "Because God made it that way." All of life is connected to God. Our fears and worries are no different.

We are God's offspring who either run from him or run to him. Those are the only two possibilities, even when we are afraid. When we are on the fence, trusting God a little and trusting ourselves a little, we can feel like we are going neither away from him nor toward him. But a closer look at our faith reveals that in our vacillating we have already made our decision: we have decided to turn from him and put our trust in ourselves or something else.

⇨ What do you think you might be saying about God when you are anxious or afraid?

The task at hand is to practice turning to the Lord when you are afraid—so it becomes natural and instinctive to turn to him. The psalmists, of course, were experts.

The LORD is my light and my salvation—
  whom shall I fear?
The LORD is the stronghold of my life—
  of whom shall I be afraid?
When evil men advance against me
  to devour my flesh,
when my enemies and my foes attack me,
  they will stumble and fall.
Though an army besiege me,
  my heart will not fear;
though war break out against me,
  even then will I be confident. (Psalm 27:1–3)

Sound impossible? Confidence even when the enemy is already in the house? At this point, it is enough to know that fear is about trust, love, and prophecies of the future, and the most important task is to learn the knack of turning quickly to the Lord.

Read Psalm 56, and notice how quickly King David moves from fear to faith:

Be merciful to me, O God, for men hotly pursue me;
  all day long they press their attack.
My slanderers pursue me all day long;
  many are attacking me in their pride.
When I am afraid,
  I will trust in you.
In God, whose word I praise,
  in God I trust; I will not be afraid.
  What can mortal man do to me?
All day long they twist my words;
  they are always plotting to harm me.
They conspire, they lurk,
  they watch my steps,
  eager to take my life.

On no account let them escape;
    in your anger, O God, bring down the nations.
Record my lament;
    list my tears on your scroll—
    are they not in your record?
Then my enemies will turn back
    when I call for help.
    By this I will know that God is for me.
In God, whose word I praise,
    in the LORD, *whose word I praise—*
in God I trust; I will not be afraid.
    What can man do to me?
I am under vows to you, O God;
    I will present my thank offerings to you.
For you have delivered me from death
    and my feet from stumbling,
that I may walk before God
    in the light of life. (Psalm 56, italics mine)

Does this discourage you or arouse hope? If it discourages you because the psalmist seems like a spiritual superman, remember that he is just like you—except you have more resources than he did. You have more of God's Word and more of the Spirit. He might be a few years ahead of you, but this psalm can be your own.

"DO NOT BE AFRAID"

Would you believe that this is the most frequent command in the Bible? More than three hundred times God commands his people to not be afraid.

There are two ways to hear these commands. One is, "Stop it right now! Don't be afraid!" In this case fear and worry would be just plain wrong. It would violate God's direct command. When afraid or anxious you would confess to the Lord that it is sin—and then confess it again and again.

But there is another way to hear this command.

Have you ever heard a parent say to a child, "Be careful"? Technically, it is a command, yet no child would take it that way. The parent is not saying, "Be careful or you will be in trouble," but, "I love you, and my desire is that you be safe."

Here is what Jesus says to you: "Do not be afraid, little flock, for your Father has been pleased to give you the kingdom" (Luke 12:32).

This is not an edict from the King. The term "little flock" gives you a window into God's heart. This is both a plea and an encouraging word from the Father, who knows and loves you. It is exactly what you need because when you are afraid you desperately need someone bigger than yourself in whom you can trust.

Are fear and worry sinful? Are they caused by a heart that doesn't trust God? Not necessarily. As you consider your fears and worries more closely, you might find that you are trusting in yourself rather than God, and in that case confession will be exactly what the doctor ordered.

No surprise there. Confession of sin is an everyday occurrence when you follow Jesus Christ, so you should expect such things when you are examining your fears. There is nothing discouraging in that. If you keep Jesus in view and give him the last word ("I have forgiven you, I do forgive you, and I will forgive you"), confession of sin will be hopeful and encouraging.

So *sometimes* you will see that your fears mean you are trusting in yourself rather than the Lord. But you will *always* find that fear and worry are opportunities to hear God, to either turn toward him or to keep facing him and grow in trusting him. "When I am afraid, I will trust in you" (Psalm 56:3).

Fear and worry are reminders. Better yet, they are opportunities. They are a string around your finger reminding you that you can trust the Creator God who hears, cares, and acts. They are opportunities to know God better.

CLOSING THOUGHTS

It's more than you bargained for, isn't it? Perhaps you picked up this workbook hoping to find a strategy that would get rid of nagging worries, but what you got is God. It is the ultimate bait and switch! You get lured in by promises of more rest in your life, but what you get is the King, the kingdom, and promises that extend beyond death.

Does that sound good? You know you are on the right path when it sounds good.

What better way to end than to pray? Given what you have considered so far, how does it lead you to pray? Go ahead and write out your prayer or have someone lead the group in prayer.

Week 1 Goals:

- To identify what your fears and anxieties predict and what they say about the Lord—deciphering that language is one of the important skills of a wise life.

- To know that because God speaks so frequently about fear and anxiety, he must care about them—no fear or anxiety seems trivial or silly to him.

- To turn more often and more quickly to the Lord when fears strike

Week 2

The God of Suspense Reveals His Plans

This week you will spend time in two Old Testament passages. They are the Bible's cornerstone for how to handle fears and anxieties. The first will be Exodus 14. Here God actually takes his people into harm's way. After 400 years they are leaving Egypt, and God tells them to take a route that will trap them so that the Egyptian army is in front of them and the inhospitable sea is behind them. But things, of course, are not always what they seem.

The second passage is from chapter 16, a little later in the Exodus story. It tells about how God gives manna to his people when they are in the desert. His intent is to teach them about fear and worry.

God does not conform to our timetable.

Our timetable, of course, is that right now our silos would be filled to the brim—with enough food for us and our descendants for the next five generations. We easily forget that such largesse would mean spiritual death for us because we would trust in our silos and have no reason to walk through life trusting our God.

> Keep falsehood and lies far from me;
> > give me neither poverty nor riches,
> > but give me only my daily bread.

Otherwise, I may have too much and disown you
    and say, "Who is the LORD?"
Or I may become poor and steal,
    and so dishonor the name of my God. (Proverbs 30:8–9)

But all the same, we would prefer that God deliver us with plenty of time to spare rather than at the eleventh hour.

DELIVERANCE AT THE ELEVENTH HOUR

The ways of God are better and wiser than our own. Although he doesn't choose last-minute deliverances every time, he assures us that this *is* one of his parenting strategies with his children. The greatest gift he could give is the gift of faith, in which we learn to trust him in good times and bad, and these deliverances can be wonderful opportunities. The person who is open to learn from them will be fearless, free, and content.

Think about it. You *will* trust in something or someone; that's part of being human. You will trust in your silos, your spouse, your wealth, your loved ones, your cunning, or your health—or you will trust in the Lord. Trust in things that are untrustworthy, and you are trusting in quicksand. You are trusting in things that cannot sustain the weight of your trust. And fear, of course, will be the result. Trust in the Lord, and you are secure.

What we need is a divine tutorial, and God often uses seemingly dire circumstances for his best tutorials.

Travel back into biblical history for a moment. The people of Israel have just been liberated from Egyptian bondage. It is one of the most important moments in the Old Testament. By God's power, and his power alone, they were leaving 400 years of slavery, and they were leaving with their sacks full of Egyptian provisions.

Then they receive a most unusual directive: God tells the people to double back *toward the Egyptians* so Pharaoh will think they are confused and vulnerable (Exodus 14:2). Smelling blood, Pharaoh pursues the trapped and defenseless Israelites. His army is in front of them, and the impassable sea is behind them. No doubt the strategy must have had Moses scratching his head, Moses' aides questioning his sanity, and the people mad—and scared.

> They said to Moses, "Was it because there were no graves in Egypt that you brought us to the desert to die? What have you done to us by bringing us out of Egypt? Didn't we say to you in Egypt, 'Leave us alone; let us serve the Egyptians'? It would have been better for us to serve the Egyptians than to die in the desert!"
> Moses answered the people, "Do not be afraid. Stand firm and you will see the deliverance the Lord will bring you today. The Egyptians you see today you will never see again. The Lord will fight for you; you need only to be still." (Exodus 14:11–14)

Stand still and watch a pivotal event in the history of Israel? That is certainly a counterintuitive directive to fearful people. Fear calls for fight and flight, not standing and watching. But in this case, as with most eleventh-hour moments, no other choice exists. They have no weapons, and there is no place to go. It is the perfect tutorial. They can only direct their saucerlike eyes to how the Lord will keep his promise to them.

Keep it, he does. The Egyptian army is destroyed, and the people walk on dry land.

> That day the Lord saved Israel from the hands of the Egyptians, and Israel saw the Egyptians lying dead on the shore. And when the Israelites saw the great power the Lord displayed against the Egyptians, the people feared the Lord and put their trust in him and in Moses his servant. (Exodus 14:30–31)

Nice deliverance, isn't it? Doesn't it make you wish that God would do such things now? But remember this: you live when God's power is even more on display than it was then. The Spirit of God has been given, and the kingdom of heaven is advancing. Somehow, you have access to an even better deliverance.

You can probably remember times when you thought everything was crashing down around you and there was no way out. Yet as you look back you can see that there *was* a way out. God guided you on a path through the trouble.

⇨ Describe a time in your life when you experienced God's deliverance.

⇨ Are there any places in your life in which you are you feeling cornered now?

Let's say you are reading a scary story or watching a scary movie. The hero is in perilous straits. Death will pounce in the next few seconds. You want to yell out, "Stop, don't do that!" But you know it's too late.

Now let's say you are reading the same book or watching the same movie, but you already know that the hero doesn't die. Though you are in the same scene as before, this time you are calm. At most, you are curious as to how your hero will be delivered, but you aren't scared because you know everything will be fine.

If you had been one of the people who were trapped by the Egyptian armies, you would, no doubt, have been overrun by fear. But once delivered, if you faced a similar situation later, you might be less scared. You might simply think, *I wonder how the Lord will deliver us this time.*

That is the story of your life when you put your trust in the King. This calmness is his desire for you. You know the ending, and you are assured that it will be good, even better than you can imagine.

Here is the choice when you face desperate situations: they can either be moments that lead you in abject terror, or they can be times when the loving Father teaches you some of the most wonderful lessons of your life.

Which perspective do you choose?

Even if you choose God's perspective, your confidence in him won't be perfect. But over time you will find that you turn to him more quickly. Someday, you might even find yourself in an impossible situation and notice that you are looking forward to what your Father will do. You will see it as an opportunity.

THE MANNA PRINCIPLE

The parting of the sea was only a warm-up.

Do you remember the passage in which Jesus tells us not to worry (Matthew 6:25–34)? He says his Father cares even for flowers and birds, which are parts of creation that are less important to him than we are. He concludes by reminding us to keep our attention on today: "Therefore do not worry about tomorrow, for tomorrow will worry about itself" (Matthew 6:34).

When he says this to us, he is thinking about the time when his Father first taught that lesson.

Jesus is thinking about manna.

It was another eleventh-hour deliverance. The children of Israel are hungry, they have no crops, and they are in the desert. Their former Egyptian slavery, even with meager rations, is starting to look better than freedom with starvation. So they respond in classic human style: with grumbling and complaining.

God counters with his characteristic holy style—because of his grace he feeds them with manna.

But the manna he sends for them to eat does more than just feed them. It also teaches them. First, it teaches them to act on the grace God gives *today* by collecting the manna and enjoying it. Second, it teaches them to trust him for *tomorrow*. Every night they go to bed with empty cupboards. Every morning they wake up wondering whether the manna will be on the ground. Every morning it is.

After about forty years of this routine, they are probably getting the hang of it. They wake up, get dressed, take out their manna pots, and head out the door before they even check to see whether the manna is there. They are learning to trust God for tomorrow.

The message is clear: act on the grace God gives you today, and wait confidently for the grace God will give you tomorrow.

Anxiety and worry are always off in the future. They are scouts on the frontier. They run ahead and spy on the enemy. When they return they tell tales of bloodthirsty giants, an enemy army that extends to the horizon, insurmountable odds, and sure defeat. These spies, you see, have been commissioned to always envision the worst-case scenario.

Your task is to denounce those alarmist spies and instead adopt the story of manna because it is, indeed, your story. Last night manna wasn't on the ground. You wake up, and there it is. It is everything you need for today.

⇨ Where in your life do you need God's manna?

⇨How could making the manna story your own change the way you live?

⇨Can you think of times when you woke up expecting the ground to be bare and he gave you just what you needed?

Can you understand why you worry when you think about tomorrow? You worry because you don't have what you need yet. If you imagine tomorrow's misery without tomorrow's manna, of course you are going to worry. Tomorrow's manna isn't on the ground yet. You have manna for today only. In his great wisdom, God doesn't give you tomorrow's manna today. Otherwise you would forget him and trust in yourself.

Get specific with your worries and anxieties. For example, let's say you are anxious about getting cancer. You have seen its effects on other people, and you fear the possible disfigurement, pain, and death. You can't imagine having grace, which is the New Testament version of manna, to go through such a thing, even though you have seen God give grace to others. You predict that tomorrow's grace will not be enough. The manna will no longer be on the ground. You worry.

But God promises grace when you need it.

What will that grace look like? The specifics are impossible to tell. But he will give you grace to trust in him, grace to love others, and *grace to have hope more than fear.*

Have you ever heard people say, in the midst of their hardships, that they can tell people are praying for them? What they are saying is, "When I imagined something like this, I always thought it would be impossible. I could never bear it. But now that I am in it, God is faithful. I can't explain it, but somehow he is carrying me along."

Now, take one of your own anxieties. Apply the manna principle to it.

⇨ Are you worried because you don't have the grace yet to deal with something that might or might not happen in the future? Like what?

Don't expect to be an expert immediately. The Israelites practiced this for forty years, and they were still clumsy when it came to trusting God during difficult times.

⇨ Any thoughts on how you can remember this story when you need it?

Fears and anxieties always want more information. They think that knowledge is power. In response, your heavenly Father confides in you. What you read in his Word is no mere story. It is the revelation of the very heart of your Father. He is bringing you into his innermost thoughts. He is giving you what your fears and anxieties are asking for. He is giving you information about the future.

THE MANNA PRINCIPLE IN ACTION

A doctor removed a suspicious mole on a man's shoulder. The doctor said he got it all but couldn't be sure until he scanned the area in another six months. Those six months were business as usual for the man. He worked, ministered to others, said little about the pending tests, and continued to pray that he would know and love the Lord. On the evening before his six-month checkup, he slept well.

The results from that checkup: his cancer had spread. The statistics indicated he had from four to twelve months to live. He had just passed the age of fifty, his junior-high-aged children were doing well, and he thought he was moving into his most productive years.

⇨ How might you have responded if you'd received this news? (Though the question is somewhat unfair because you do not have manna for such things right now.)

This man's actual response? After hearing the death sentence, his first words were, "Nothing has changed."

In other words, God had rained manna yesterday and today, and he would send it tomorrow. God is good now, and he will be good tomorrow. This man believed that God could deliver him from cancer—but whether he did or not, God was still God, God would give the even better deliverance, and the man would trust him.

Many tears followed but very few fears or worries. He had been trained in his Father's schoolroom over the years, and he had listened well.

Do you aspire to such a response?

It is possible. Even better, you should *expect* the Father to do this kind of powerful work in your own heart.

Here are some other people who knew the manna principle.

> Shadrach, Meshach and Abednego replied to the king, "O
> Nebuchadnezzar, we do not need to defend ourselves before you

in this matter. If we are thrown into the blazing furnace, the God we serve is able to save us from it, and he will rescue us from your hand, O king. But even if he does not, we want you to know, O king, that we will not serve your gods or worship the image of gold you have set up." (Daniel 3:16–18)

Shadrach, Meshach, and Abednego are Jewish teenagers. They are captives with many of their countrymen in Babylon. These three had been selected to be treated specially by the king to see whether they might prove useful as advisors.

They are ordinary young men living in exile before the time when the Spirit of God is poured out. They have never actually seen God deliver anyone. They have only read about his goodness and power, in the Exodus story. But that is enough for them to be confident that their God reigns over the rulers of the world and gives grace to his people when they need it.

Notice how they apply the Exodus story. They believe that God certainly *can* deliver them from the furnace, but they also know that he can have other plans for them that do not include immediate deliverance. What they know for certain is this:

- We trust in God not because he delivers us from every fearful situation, but because he alone is King.
- He will always be with us in fearful situations.
- He will deliver his people, but at times his deliverance will be more sophisticated than we can understand. We might have hope that he delivers us from a negative job review with a supervisor, while he is actually doing a cosmic deliverance that will include all creation.

These three Hebrew men anticipate death by fire, which must be at the top of anyone's worst nightmare list.

Their response? They simply trust God.

God might bring deliverance that saves you from your present difficulty, but he might not. You don't trust in deliverance; you trust in God.

⇨ Do you think such trust is possible? Don't forget, these three men did not yet have the Spirit of God in the way that you do.

At this point, you know one thing for certain: God will give you grace when you need it. You can't imagine being thrown into the fire. If you tried, you might think that if it were to happen your fear would be so intense that you might die before you even saw the flames, which, of course, is what you would prefer. But God promises to give you grace if such a thing were to ever happen to you, and that grace would be much better than what you can imagine.

In fact, don't even bother to imagine it because you can't. You don't have the grace yet. That will come on another day.

Let the manna principle lead you in prayer. Start with thanks because he has delivered you and will deliver you. And, while you are at it, you could also confess how, in your fears and anxieties, you are a false prophet.

Here is a different prophecy, and it can become your desire:

> When I am afraid,
>   I will trust in you.
> In God, whose word I praise,
>   in God I trust; I will not be afraid.
>   What can mortal man do to me? (Psalm 56:3–4)

Keep Psalm 56 in mind as you write out a prayer of confession and trust to your heavenly Father.

Week 2 Goals:

- To know that God gives a *better* deliverance

- To be able to give examples of a better deliverance

- To make the manna story *your* story

- To be able to give examples of what form manna, or grace, can take

Week 3

The King Comes Close and Talks about Money

This week you'll go from Exodus to the Sermon on the Mount. The story about manna will still be in view, but Jesus will adorn it even more when he says to you, "Do not worry about your life, what you will eat; or about your body, what you will wear" (Luke 12:22). Fear and your money are the targets this time.

This week, consider a familiar passage from the part of the Sermon on the Mount in which Jesus says, "Do not worry." But first read the introduction to these well-known words. The worry he is specifically addressing is about money, and it is all built on the manna story.

> Then [Jesus] said to them, "Watch out! Be on your guard against all kinds of greed; a man's life does not consist in the abundance of his possessions."
>
> And he told them this parable: "The ground of a certain rich man produced a good crop. He thought to himself, 'What shall I do? I have no place to store my crops.'
>
> "Then he said, 'This is what I'll do. I will tear down my barns and build bigger ones, and there I will store all my grain and my goods. And I'll say to myself, "You have plenty of good things laid up for many years. Take life easy; eat, drink and be merry."'

"But God said to him, 'You fool! This very night your life will be demanded from you. Then who will get what you have prepared for yourself?'

"This is how it will be with anyone who stores up things for himself but is not rich toward God."

Then Jesus said to his disciples: "Therefore I tell you, do not worry about your life, what you will eat; or about your body, what you will wear. Life is more than food, and the body more than clothes." (Luke 12:15–23)

In the manna story, Moses was speaking. Now it is Jesus speaking. God is getting personal with you. The one who spoke those words on a hillside in Palestine is the same Lord who has risen and still speaks to you by the Spirit. It is enough to make you want to really listen.

JESUS SPEAKS TO YOU ABOUT GREED

His words begin with the warning, "Watch out!" Could one of the reasons you worry be that you love possessions and you want more? We love our things, and we are anxious when something we love is threatened.

Greed lives in every human heart.

What keeps you from hearing warnings about greed? Jesus explains it like this: "The worries of this life, the deceitfulness of wealth and the desires for other things come in and choke the word, making it unfruitful" (Mark 4:19).

This is something to worry about. The deceitfulness of wealth plugs your ears to warnings about the deceitfulness of wealth. Yes, that is reason to be scared.

But shouldn't you care about your financial needs?

Absolutely. Jesus cares too. He was speaking with compassion to a community that, for the most part, was very poor by today's standards, and, if they chose to follow Jesus, they would probably slip further down the economic ladder. But greed is unrelated to the size of our bank accounts. Greed is about our *wants*. Because these wants—these things we love—can be deceitful and hide, you need to bring as many of them out into the open as you can.

⇨What money-related things do you love that bring anxiety? Specifically, which ones cause you to worry when you think about losing them? Vacations? Cars? Money for hobbies? Personal security? Comfort?

Be prepared to find mixed allegiances. Greed says that God is not generous. It reveals that we are more interested in our own kingdom than in God's. That is serious, but if you see that in yourself, be encouraged. Such a response means that you are listening to Jesus' warning about greed and that the Spirit is at work. Sin is never good, but it is good to have your false allegiances exposed so you can turn from them.

JESUS WANTS TO PERSUADE YOU

Another reason to be encouraged is that the King speaks to you as your Father. He speaks beautiful words that woo you to himself, more than edicts to which you must blindly submit.

Listen as Jesus woos you away from your worries:

> "Do not worry about your life, what you will eat; or about
> your body, what you will wear. Life is more than food, and the
> body more than clothes. Consider the ravens: They do not sow
> or reap, they have no storeroom or barn; yet God feeds them.

And how much more valuable you are than birds! Who of you by worrying can add a single hour to his life? Since you cannot do this very little thing, why do you worry about the rest?

"Consider how the lilies grow. They do not labor or spin. Yet I tell you, not even Solomon in all his splendor was dressed like one of these. If that is how God clothes the grass of the field, which is here today, and tomorrow is thrown into the fire, how much more will he clothe you, O you of little faith! And do not set your heart on what you will eat or drink; do not worry about it. For the pagan world runs after all such things, and your Father knows that you need them. But seek his kingdom, and these things will be given to you as well." (Luke 12:22–31)

Go slowly on this. You already know it, but God's Word always yields more of its riches to those who diligently mine it.

"Life is more than food," Jesus says, "and the body more than clothes" (Luke 12:23). Jesus is reminding you that there is something more important than new toys and possessions. Take away all your things, and you are still a living, breathing, gifted person. Life *must* be about more than what money can buy.

⇨ What is Jesus talking about? What is better than possessions?

⇨Do you really think that these things are better than possessions? Explain.

Jesus isn't done. He makes his case, layering one appeal upon another. "Consider the ravens: They do not sow or reap, they have no storeroom or barn; yet God feeds them. And how much more valuable you are than birds!" (Luke 12:24).

The assumption is that ravens—common, ordinary birds—are well cared for. And they are. They are the ultimate survivors. You simply don't have to worry about the ravens in the neighborhood going hungry.

God cares for a bird that is neither particularly attractive nor unique. If God cares for ravens, he will surely care for you, one who is made in God's image. You are God's offspring in a way that ravens are not. You call God your Father; they don't. Your Father certainly is more concerned about the details of your life than a raven's.

And then with a wink Jesus essentially says, "It should be a little humbling for you to learn wisdom from a common bird. They don't amass riches, and yet they do fine. Why would you, child of God, amass riches?"

⇨ What are some material things that you want? (Just list the top five!)

⇨ How does knowing that your heavenly Father is caring for you change the way you view what you want?

Jesus' loving arguments are piling up. He obviously cares about your worries. Why else would he keep working to persuade you?

"Who of you by worrying can add a single hour to his life?
Since you cannot do this very little thing, why do you worry
about the rest?" (Luke 12:25)

Your Father gives life and takes it. You don't have the power to take one more step beyond what your Father gives you. Sure, you can eat well, exercise, avoid motorcycles, and wear sunblock, but you know that those precautions can't promise an extra hour of life.

⇨ Jesus' words here are deep. Think about your financial worries. How could applying Jesus' words change your thinking?

Jesus is far from done. Next, he draws your attention to a common daylily, which no one planted or tends and that has no eternal significance, and yet it is adorned with beauty.

A glance at creation tells you that Jesus cares about beauty. How he developed a reputation as a no-frills, function-before-beauty rabbi is hard to understand. It may have fit John the Baptist but not Jesus. Jesus is on a mission to beautify the world.

Are you concerned about your appearance? You must have forgotten that our heavenly Father cares for more than our basic needs. He is serving you with the ultimate beauty treatments. He is preparing you to be his bride.

⇨ Are you persuaded that being part of God's kingdom is better than building your own kingdom? If not, what keeps Jesus' words from penetrating your heart? (Check for greed!)

If we are unmoved, Jesus identifies our dilemma this way: "O you of little faith!" We divide faith into portions. We take a percentage and invest it in the world, and whatever is left we invest in the kingdom of God. For some things, such as our eternal destiny, we trust Jesus, but for others, such as money and the long list of other items we love, we reserve the right to make our own decisions. "Little faith" means that our hearts are set on our own desires rather than on our Father's care.

Fear and worry can reveal the things that we love.

⇨ Do you divvy up your faith? When or for what do you trust the Lord, and when or for what do you trust yourself?

⇨ Can you imagine what it would be like to trust your heavenly Father with your whole heart? Describe what that might look like.

Jesus is not quite finished:

> "And do not set your heart on what you will eat or drink; do
> not worry about it. For the pagan world runs after all such things,
> and your Father knows that you need them." (Luke 12:29–30)

To paraphrase, "You are acting just like people in the world around you. They live like orphans who have no father to take care of them. It is one thing to be a street kid who lives by his wits because there is no one else who watches out for him. If such a child hoards pennies, steals when he can, and obsesses about whether or not he will find his next meal, you can understand. But when your Father is the King who has all the wealth of the land and loves you dearly, such behavior looks insane and is a grief to your Father."

Then Jesus summarizes his appeal to you. Don't act like orphans, he says, but seek the kingdom: "Seek his kingdom, and these things will be given to you as well" (Luke 12:31).

JESUS OFFERS THE KINGDOM

This is a good deal. When you turn away from securing your own kingdom, which teeters on bankruptcy anyway, you get the *true* kingdom.

Know the kingdom and seek it. That is the alternative to worry.

This kingdom was inaugurated with power after the death and resurrection of Jesus Christ, whose name literally means "Jesus the King." Those events were so fundamental and conclusive that the Father has determined that entry to the kingdom will be solely on the basis of Jesus. He is the door. Membership is not based on race, nationality, or even your efforts to abide by the King's law. The evidence of membership is that you believe Jesus died for your sins and was raised from the dead, and you now put your trust in the reigning King rather than in yourself.

With the perfect and powerful King now on the throne, his reign will progress subtly but inexorably. Nothing will ever stop it. If you are part of it, the kingdom can never be taken away from you.

The kingdom is where Jesus reigns. The kingdom is where all God's promises are guaranteed or already fulfilled. It is with you now.

Think of what the Spirit, who is the presence of Jesus Christ, has given you:

- Forgiveness
- A new heart
- Adoption as his child
- Power to be more like Jesus
- Unfailing love
- The presence of the King
- A mission
- Security
- Resurrection
- Unity with God
- Unity with other people
- Justice
- Mercy
- Rest
- Peace
- Righteousness
- Joy

These are called spiritual blessings. Keep in mind that "spiritual" means they are given by the Spirit, not that they are imaginary or only reside in the distant future. *The* kingdom is actually *more* real than your day-to-day world because this world, however attractive it may be at times, is passing away. Like a once-glorious house, it will not last. It is not eternal. But spiritual blessings are permanent (see 1 Peter 1:3–9).

Jesus ends his appeal to you this way:

> Do not be afraid, little flock, for your Father has been pleased to give you the kingdom. Sell your possessions and give to the poor. Provide purses for yourselves that will not wear out, a treasure in heaven that will not be exhausted, where no thief comes near and no moth destroys. For where your treasure is, there your heart will be also. (Luke 12:32–34)

Beautiful, isn't it? Gentle, generous, persuasive. It is too good to read quickly and move on to other things.

⇨ What is Jesus saying to you in this teaching? What will you do in response?

⇨ Do you give regularly to the church? That is one very specific way to test yourself and see if there are more financial fears than you think.

⇨ How will you pray because of these words from Jesus? Don't forget about confessing dual allegiances.

Week 3 Goals:

- To be able to paraphrase, in your own words, why Jesus says you don't have to be anxious about money

- To identify what your anxieties about money say about your desires (that they are too great) and your God (that he is stingy)

- To be able to describe *the* kingdom

Week 4

The Living God Speaks about Death

The first common fear you have looked at is the worry that you will not have enough money. The next is the ever-present fear of death.

You might think that followers of Jesus Christ, who are certain of the resurrection, would be inoculated against this fear, but you are not. All you have to do is imagine how your life would be different without any traces of the fear of death, and you will find that it still courses through your veins. What would you do or stop doing if you knew you would not die?

This fear doesn't have to cripple you though. The Truths this week will speak to the fear of death.

One mark of Christ's true followers is that they face the reality of death because of their faith. Another is that they can face it with fearlessness.

The twelve disciples fall apart when Jesus is taken into custody. Without their leader, they scatter. Peter's fear of death is singled out as a particularly dramatic one—for fear of his life he denies even knowing Jesus. Of course, most of the other disciples would have done the same given similar circumstances. Give Peter some credit for at least following Jesus to the scene of his trial.

Something happens to a man when he has witnessed someone rise from the dead. Even more, something happens once the Spirit of Christ dwells within him.

For Peter and the other disciples, that transformation occurs immediately. One day they are hiding behind locked doors, the next they are preaching about Jesus in the temple courts—where it is likely that they will be treated just like their master had been and condemned to death. For the rest of us, that transition from fear of death to fearlessness usually takes more time.

Solomon wrote: "It is better to go to a house of mourning than to go to a house of feasting, for death is the destiny of every man; the living should take this to heart" (Ecclesiastes 7:2).

To face "the destiny of every man" is a task you naturally postpone. But, like fear itself, when you know that good answers exist to a disagreeable problem, you are more eager to tackle it. And if there are answers to anything in the Bible, it is to the fear of death.

FEAR OF *HOW* YOU MIGHT DIE

Let's start with fears about the *way* you could die. Until recently, the descent into death was a quick one. Now, it can be prolonged so that a long, slow demise is a fear that has seeped into the national consciousness. Not that a slow death is necessarily worse than a speedy one because there is no good way to die, but a slow death can be more painful.

An otherwise healthy man goes for a yearly checkup and hears that his PSA level is elevated. It might mean nothing. More tests will tell, but his mind immediately remembers friends who had prostate surgery and lost sexual functioning. Then he remembers the older man in his church whose prostate cancer dogged him for fifteen years before finally taking his life.

For women who have abnormal mammograms, the threat is even worse. If you have made it to middle age, you have already lost a friend to breast cancer. You know that this kind of cancer seems to tease you with occasional good news while the fight against it becomes a full-time, painful job.

And what about Alzheimer's disease, strokes, and illnesses that could force you to be dependent on others? You can't like the thought of being cared for by your children—or worse, by an anonymous nursing home staff.

At first glance, the Psalms seem to be little help. So many psalms speak with confidence about deliverance, but you feel it would be presumptuous to claim that deliverance as your own. This is a different era, after all. No longer does God bring glory to himself by a human kingdom that stands for his righteousness against the surrounding idolatry. Now he brings glory to himself by allowing the church to multiply, sometimes through the suffering of many of its people.

When the Cross became the pivotal point in human history, the definition of deliverance changed. It had once meant temporal deliverance from neighboring marauders. Now it means that you could die for the cause of Christ but still be delivered from the worse or "second" death.

God certainly does heal his people, sometimes in miraculous ways; but unless the return of Jesus intervenes, you, all of us, *will* die. If the disease from which you were healed doesn't take your life, another one will.

Feeling better yet?

Believe it or not, you should be. While the rest of the world would be breaking out into a cold sweat at the thought of such things, you can have a growing confidence that you will have grace to deal with those difficulties if, indeed, they come to pass.

Manna. Just think manna. Today you do not have the manna—the grace—to endure what could come in the future. Even thinking about how you could die should give you a mild case of the willies. But whatever happens tomorrow, you will have all the manna you need. Tomorrow. God gives you what you need for today, not tomorrow.

⇨ You can't predict what form that manna will take because God is in the habit of giving better than what you think. But what do you think that manna could look like when your body is wasting away?

⇨ Who do you know who has found grace despite physical disability? You might want to talk to someone who has demonstrated unwavering faith during sickness. Ask such people how God's grace and mercy found them at their most difficult times.

FEAR OF JUDGMENT

Just as you begin to learn how to trust God for *how* you will die, you have to face some kind of judgment day.

This should spark some interesting discussions.

Most people who are intimately familiar with fear or anxiety are quite aware that a judgment day is coming. Fearful people tend to be scrupulous about their sins. They know they have done wrong before God, and they take that wrong seriously. They don't need the Bible to persuade them that a reckoning is ahead.

The only way you can deny the coming judgment is if you use the cut-and-paste method of reading the Bible. Here are some of the passages that assume such a day:

- "I tell you that men will have to give account on the day of judgment for every careless word they have spoken" (Matthew 12:36).

- As Paul discoursed on righteousness, self-control, and the judgment to come, Felix was afraid and said, "That's enough for now! You may leave. When I find it convenient, I will send for you" (Acts 24:25).
- "You, then, why do you judge your brother? Or why do you look down on your brother? For we will all stand before God's judgment seat. It is written: 'As surely as I live,' says the Lord, 'every knee will bow before me; every tongue will confess to God.' So then, each of us will give an account of himself to God" (Romans 14:10–12).
- Man is destined to die once, and after that to face judgment (Hebrews 9:27).

There are no exceptions. Everyone appears before the King. It's enough to leave you a little wobbly in the knees. You have sinned, and you will appear before God on a day of judgment. No wonder Freud observed a "free-floating anxiety" that seemed to hover over humanity.

We will all appear before the bar, of that there is no doubt. Yet we will not all come in the same way. If you have avoided Jesus Christ and have put your faith in yourself and things that don't last, you will appear before the judgment on your own, with no one in your corner. That is not a threat. It is simply what lies at the end of a path of self-focused allegiances. The result will be the ultimate isolation. You will stand before the Lord of the universe accused, utterly defenseless, without an advocate.

If you have put your faith in Jesus, one of the benefits of that decision is forgiveness of sins—and sins are the only thing that can separate you from God. Such a person does not go alone, to anything, ever—especially to the judgment.

Here is one way that the apostle Paul describes what Jesus did at the Cross:

> Judgment followed one sin [Adam's sin] and brought condemnation, but the gift [of eternal life and no condemnation from Jesus] followed many trespasses and brought justification. For if, by the trespass of the one man, death reigned through that one man, how much more will those who receive God's abundant provision of grace and of the gift of righteousness reign in life through the one man, Jesus Christ.

Consequently, just as the result of one trespass was condemnation for all men, so also the result of one act of righteousness was justification that brings life for all men. For just as through the disobedience of the one man the many were made sinners, so also through the obedience of the one man the many will be made righteous. (Romans 5:16–19)

This gets to the very heart of the good news you have received through Jesus. Nothing is more important that you could know. In it resides God's response to the fear of death, but it is a mouthful.

⇨ How would you explain this in your own words? What is Paul saying?

The King himself has taken your punishment (Hebrews 9:27–28). There is no punishment left to mete out to you. Even more, he gives you his Spirit, who in turn gives you power to live for the King rather than for yourself. Yet it is not your obedience that earns your freedom from punishment. Your obedience is the evidence that you have been liberated.

When a man works, his wages are not credited to him as a gift, but as an obligation. However, to the man who does not work but trusts God who justifies the wicked, his faith is credited as righteousness. (Romans 4:4–5)

You still don't have all the details. You don't know precisely how these passages square with a day of judgment. What you do know, however, is very good news. The primary emotion you will experience in heaven is joy. If your works are evaluated, that evaluation will lessen neither God's love for you nor your joy in him.

Just one more question. Many Christians believe they won't be condemned, but they believe they won't be *commended* either. Instead of "Well done, good and faithful servant," many Christians believe that the day of judgment will expose their many failures. If you believe this is your future, you will be anxious.

⇨ What would you say about this?

At the risk of belaboring the day of judgment, one more detail is too easily overlooked. It is this: when you see him there will be manna—new grace available to you. And you know exactly what that manna will look like: when you see him, you will be like him (1 John 3:2).

One thing that means is that you will have no more tears or sorrow, no more aches and pains. But more importantly it means that you will be without sin. You will know his love more clearly, and you will love him perfectly.

It looks like this. Consider one of the worst scenarios for a Christian. You die. At the judgment it is revealed that you have not exactly been a paragon of Christian virtue. Others are ushered to their mansions while you are shown a clean but humble one-bedroom efficiency. Not a bad worst-case scenario.

But the real story is different. When you see the Lord face-to-face, you will love him with all your heart. You will be given the bread of life. Your soul will be deeply satisfied. At that moment you will have the best—you will desire nothing else. No matter what kind of judgment he makes, you will be amazed. Because you will be like him, you will be in sync with what he says. Even if your apartment scenario is remotely accurate, you will have perfect contentment, regardless of your address.

Those folks who got mansions? Because you love them, you will not covet or be jealous. Instead, you will be excited for them.

And one other detail. Because you are united with the new owners, what is theirs is yours anyway.

This scenario is, of course, a false prophecy. The Bible never suggests that there will be a heavenly ghetto. But it does show how God's Word can bring hope even to your worst-case fears.

⇨ When you know you have the manna that comes with sinlessness awaiting you, you can pray with thanksgiving. Write out a prayer of thanksgiving, asking God to fill you with hope, instead of fear, as you think about death.

Week 4 Goals:

- To face even your worst fears

- To face your worst fears knowing that you will receive manna when you need it

- To understand that hope is the opposite of fear. Hope is a prediction that God will be good

Week 5

The Loving Father Woos You from the Fear of Man

So far you have considered the fear of financial loss and the fear of death. Now you will go face-to-face with the fear of *other people*. The Bible calls it the fear of man.

The Bible highlights three primary fears: fear of death, fear of financial ruin, and fear of other people. Of the three, the fear of other people can be the most subtle and menacing.[1] "Fear of man will prove to be a snare, but whoever trusts in the Lord is kept safe" (Proverbs 29:25).

You can find the fear of man everywhere:

- Have you ever struggled with peer pressure?
- Have you ever been overly concerned about your appearance?
- Have you ever been tempted to get plastic surgery?
- Do you find that your view of yourself fluctuates on the basis of your achievements or the opinions of others?
- Do you show favoritism?
- Do you ever say yes when you should say no?
- Do your public actions look much better than your private thoughts and behaviors?
- Have you ever had a difficult time loving someone because you didn't feel loved by that person?

---

1. More in-depth material on the fear of other people can be found in my book *When People Are Big and God Is Small*.

- Do you ever struggle with jealousy?
- Have you ever been scared to talk about Jesus with someone for fear that the person would think differently of you?

If you said yes to any of these questions, you are acquainted with the fear of man. When you fear something, you allow it to control you. When you fear other people, you allow them to control you. Their opinions, possible opinions, attitudes, or withholding of love become your master.

GRASSHOPPERS AMONG GIANTS

The human instinct of fear has a long history. It was the culprit when the Israelites left Egypt and were right on the border of the land God had promised them. At that time the Hebrew spies who searched out the land gave Moses this report:

> "We went into the land to which you sent us, and it does flow with milk and honey! Here is its fruit. But the people who live there are powerful, and the cities are fortified and very large. We even saw descendants of Anak there. The Amalekites live in the Negev; the Hittites, Jebusites and Amorites live in the hill country; and the Canaanites live near the sea and along the Jordan."
>
> Then Caleb silenced the people before Moses and said, "We should go up and take possession of the land, for we can certainly do it."
>
> But the men who had gone up with him said, "We can't attack those people; they are stronger than we are." And they spread among the Israelites a bad report about the land they had explored. They said, "The land we explored devours those living in it. All the people we saw there are of great size. We saw the Nephilim there (the descendants of Anak come from the Nephilim). We seemed like grasshoppers in our own eyes, and we looked the same to them." (Numbers 13:27–33)

The people had just watched God conquer the powerful Egyptian army, and they'd never even sharpened their swords. Led by such a mighty God, they are invincible. Everyone *else* should feel like grasshoppers, but the spies are controlled by the fear of what other people could do to them. Their report is silly and foolish. Worse, it is just plain sinful. It is evidence that they didn't trust the God who delivers.

Fearing people, being controlled by people, or putting your trust in people—they are all the same thing.

> This is what the LORD says:
> "Cursed is the one who trusts in man,
>   who depends on flesh for his strength
>   and whose heart turns away from the LORD.
> He will be like a bush in the wastelands;
>   he will not see prosperity when it comes.
> He will dwell in the parched places of the desert,
>   in a salt land where no one lives.
> But blessed is the man who trusts in the LORD,
>   whose confidence is in him.
> He will be like a tree planted by the water
>   that sends out its roots by the stream.
> It does not fear when heat comes;
>   its leaves are always green.
> It has no worries in a year of drought
>   and never fails to bear fruit." (Jeremiah 17:5–8)

⇨ Can you think of other stories in the Bible where people put their trust in people rather than the Lord?

⇨ Where in your own life do you allow other people to control you? In what ways do you fear them, need something from them, or put your trust in them?

Today we are less threatened by enemies that could kill us. We fear others not because they can injure us physically, but because they might not like, love, or respect us. Certainly, nothing is wrong with desiring love or respect from other people. In fact, to not desire it would be a sign that something is very wrong. And we *should* be affected by what other people say. But there are times when we allow other people to control us more than we allow God to control us.

LOVE EXPELS FEAR

When clear answers to difficult problems such as this one are elusive, when in doubt, love.

In the case of the fear of man, love and fear don't mix. Love expels fear.

Children don't fear parents who love them. Even when they have done wrong and they know it, children might hang their head when they face the one who loves them, but they are not afraid. They know they won't be shamed or rejected. Now add to this scenario a child who responds to parental love by loving the parents in return.

The principle is clear: you can't fear someone who loves you and whom you love.

God's Love for You Expels Fear

Do you know you are loved by someone? Do you know you are loved because the other person loves you and not because you are so lovable?

"Why do you love me?" a wife asks her husband. A wise husband thinks carefully before he responds. *Why is she asking this?* One reason for the question could be that she doesn't feel very lovable at the moment. In other words, she may be asking, "What is it about me that you love because I am not finding too much about me that is praiseworthy at this particular moment?"

"I love you because you are so kind." Good answer but not great.

"I love you because you are beautiful inside and out." Better answer, but it, too, will fall short because what if she ages and becomes less beautiful? Half the reasons you love her have just been erased by the appearance of a few wrinkles and a dozen extra pounds. And what about those days when she is cranky? Worse yet, what if the cranky and less attractive days coincide?

The best answer is, "*I love you because I love you.* I love you when you are cranky, when you are a saint, when you are beautiful, and when you are . . . not up to your normal standards of beauty. I just love you."

At first it is a mild blow to her ego. The husband loves her yet not because of any particular trait within her. Still, could there be a better answer? He's saying that no matter what the external circumstances, he will love her. She will be loved when she is good and when she is bad.

That is the gospel.

God took all the initiative. He loved you while you were an enemy of his. He loves you now not because you are great, but because he is love. Such love is unwavering and secure. The Cross of Jesus—the ultimate evidence of God's love—establishes it.

Go ahead; try doubting the Lord's self-sacrificing love revealed at the Cross. You can't do it.

Remember, he loves you because he is love. That is humbling and wonderful.

⇨ Do you believe this? Or let me ask it from a different angle: how do your actions and fears show that you don't *really* believe it?

Loving Others More Expels Fear

The world you live in is unbalanced. In other words, you are loved more than you love. As a result, your goal should be to align yourself with that divine strategy. Your goal is to love other people more than you want to be loved by them.

It sounds unfair at first, but think of it. Yes, we all want to be loved, but imagine what it would be like to desire to love more than to be loved, even if the one outweighs the other by only a fraction.

⇨ What are some examples of ways you could love more than you seek love? What situations or relationships come to mind in which you or someone else is seeking to be loved more than seeking to love others?

⇨If you were to employ this divine strategy in your own life, how would the opinions of other people become less controlling?

FEAR AND SHAME

To give more love than you are trying to receive is always good, and it can usually break the spell of the fear of man. The problem can be a bit trickier, however, when fear is coupled with shame. Shame can confuse relationships and leave people feeling worthless and dominated by others.

You should be on guard if you use any of these words to describe you:

- Unwanted
- Defiled
- Abandoned
- Rejected
- Contaminated
- Unclean
- Shunned
- Exposed

You will find shame when your sins are made public. Sexual sins are the most common: adultery, pornography, homosexuality, even pregnancy outside of marriage (though that sin is seen as less shameful today). Lying about something important, embezzlement, and plagiarism are other examples. If your faults have ever been exposed and you wanted to run away and hide, you are familiar with shame.

Everyone acknowledges some sins—gossip, selfishness, or anger, for example. Even preachers will admit to them. Church leaders can acknowledge sexual lust in their hearts (though not in their behavior) and not experience shame. Yet every culture has an implicit list of behaviors—taboos—that are considered shameful. When it is revealed that you have done them, other people will avoid eye contact. Walk in the room and conversations stop. You feel isolated and dirty.

There is another way to experience shame too. Many times shame is a result of what you do, as stated above. But at other times shame comes from what has been done to you. Rejection or abandonment by parents or a spouse, any sexual violation, or being closely related to someone whose shameful behavior was made public can all bring shame. Some adults can even feel shame if they were adopted as children.

The problem is that confession of sin, cleansing from guilt, and even loving other people don't always remove shame. Shame needs another form of treatment.

The Old Testament is very familiar with shame. The book of Leviticus, for example, lists clear guidelines for what to do in cases of shame and defilement. In that day, if a person were unclean or shamed, others in the community exiled him until he was considered cleansed, which came by making sacrifices or bathing in a way God prescribed. Those considered ritually pure had to avoid anyone who had been shamed or defiled, or they would become defiled themselves. What they had could be caught.

When Jesus entered history, everything changed, including the prescription for shame. Any other rabbi such as him would have never associated with unclean people, but Jesus seemed to *prefer* them. He searched out the demon-possessed, lepers, and prostitutes.

Shame-filled people, when they really know Jesus, want to move toward him.

Now one of the Pharisees invited Jesus to have dinner with
him, so he went to the Pharisee's house and reclined at the table.

When a woman who had lived a sinful life in that town learned that Jesus was eating at the Pharisee's house, she brought an alabaster jar of perfume, and as she stood behind him at his feet weeping, she began to wet his feet with her tears. Then she wiped them with her hair, kissed them and poured perfume on them.

When the Pharisee who had invited him saw this, he said to himself, "If this man were a prophet, he would know who is touching him and what kind of woman she is—that she is a sinner." (Luke 7:36–39)

Like fear, shame can make us want to run and hide. But not when the shamed person really knows Jesus. This woman had seen Jesus in action and knew that he invited outcasts and unclean people to himself. She wanted to move *toward* him.

⇨ Do you believe that about Jesus? Do you really know it personally? Describe how your shame makes you want to hide from people—and perhaps run toward Christ.

Lots of action is behind the scenes in this story about the woman kissing Jesus' feet (also see Luke 8:42–48). Whenever Jesus touched, or was touched by, someone unclean, power flowed out of him. In that purposeful touch, Jesus took the shame of the person onto himself, while simultaneously passing his holiness onto the unclean person. Unclean people make clean people unclean, but the Holy One makes unclean people clean.

That's what happened at the Cross. When you trust in him rather than in yourself, by faith you are brought into contact with him. You touch him and are touched by him. In that touch a transfer takes place. Jesus takes your guilt and shame and in return gives you his righteousness.

Even if you don't experience shame, all this should make you very hopeful, especially considering any fears of condemnation you may have. Because Jesus invites the unclean and defiled to himself, he certainly invites you.

We are still talking about fear and worry. Here is the connection: one of the most important things Jesus will ever say to you is, "I am with you." That is the treatment for fear, and the only thing that could jeopardize his presence is your sin and shame. If he has dealt with that problem, you never have to fear that he will leave you.

⇨ Write out your prayer for this week's lesson. You could confess sin because you know it can separate you from the Lord, and you know that he forgives because he is the forgiving God. You could bring ways you have been shamed to the Lord because you know that he seeks you out and touches you. What is on your heart?

Week 5 Goals:

- To identify your fear of other people

- To be able to make the connection between fearing people, needing what people can give you, and loving what other people can give you more than loving God

- To be able to imagine the freedom that comes when the fear of man leaves—that freedom, rather than detaching you from others, allows you to love more deeply.

- To grow in your desire for unbalanced love

Week 6

The God of Hope Keeps His Promises

Fear and anxiety are more confident than they should be. They are *certain* that bad things will happen and that there will not be sufficient grace when they come. In response, the Lord speaks his greatest promise: "I will never leave you." Then he repeats it. Then he swears to it.

It is two days before Christmas. You place an online order for the perfect present for someone you love. Later that day you call to check the status of the order, and you actually get to speak to someone. The package is at a regional depot and the weather is getting worse, but the person on the phone promises that it will be there by 10:00 a.m. the next day. He promises, and he says that if there is any problem he will drive it there personally. With that kind of assurance—even though it is from an anonymous person—your worries cease.

If a promise from a mere human can ease your concerns, how much more can the promises that God makes? This week you will find that God goes to extremes to assure you that he will keep his promise to you. And his promise is, "I will be with you."

"I WILL BE WITH YOU"

Fear and anxiety feel so alone. Anxiety loves it when someone else helps shoulder the burden. Fear yearns for someone bigger, smarter, and stronger to turn back the threat.

When the director of a scary movie wants to really give you the creeps, the hero will be led into danger *alone*. Even Jesus' agonizing moments seemed to intensify because he was completely alone. No disciples were awake even to pray.

If only you could have a companion—the right companion—at the height of your worries or fears, then everything would be different.

⇨ Describe a time when having human companionship lessened your fears and anxieties.

Isaac is afraid. This Old Testament patriarch is troubled because everywhere he had gone he had gotten into disputes over water rights. Water rights are very important for sheepherders, so it is natural for him to be afraid. In response, God tells him that he will be with him: "I am the God of your father Abraham. Do not be afraid, for I am with you" (Genesis 26:24). For Isaac, that means water. For us it means living water.

Jacob, Isaac's son, is afraid. He is on his own in a strange country. Meanwhile, at home he had antagonized his brother Esau to the point where Jacob wonders whether he can ever return. In response, God says that he will be with him, and that means God will be faithful to any promises he had made. "I am with you and will watch over you wherever you go, and I will bring you back to this land. I will not leave you until I have done what I have promised you." (Genesis 28:15)

The Israelites had rebelled against the Lord by worshipping an idol. But because God had made promises to the people's forefathers, he is still going to take them out of the desert and give them their own land.

> Then the LORD said to Moses, "Leave this place, you and the people you brought up out of Egypt, and go up to the land I promised on oath to Abraham, Isaac and Jacob, saying, 'I will give it to your descendants.' I will send an angel before you and drive out the Canaanites, Amorites, Hittites, Perizzites, Hivites and Jebusites." (Exodus 33:1–2)

Did you notice the small but significant change in what the Lord said? He will send an angel—not himself, just an angel. That, of course, is not enough for Moses. There are too many enemies, too much to fear. Without the Lord's very presence, Moses isn't going to budge.

Some might call it obstinacy, but the Lord is pleased that Moses won't settle for anything less than the presence of God, so he reassures Moses that he will be faithful to his promise:

> The LORD replied, "My Presence will go with you, and I will give you rest."
> Then Moses said to him, "If your Presence does not go with us, do not send us up from here. How will anyone know that you are pleased with me and with your people unless you go with us? What else will distinguish me and your people from all the other people on the face of the earth?" (Exodus 33:14–16)

Moses' request for the most important thing—the Presence—marks him as the greatest leader Israel will have before Jesus. So when Joshua is called to follow Moses and lead a large group that has renegade tendencies, he feels inadequate and, no doubt, afraid.

The pattern is now clear. The Lord hears fearful people and encourages them by being faithful to his greatest promise. God tells Joshua he will be with him: "Be strong and courageous. Do not be terrified; do not be discouraged, for the LORD your God will be with you wherever you go" (Joshua 1:9).

"Be strong and courageous." A phrase like that, just dangling on its own, doesn't work. You can't simply command a frightened person to be strong and courageous, and expect a transformation. What makes the command work is this part: "God will be with you wherever you go."

When you search the Bible and find exhortations to not worry or be afraid, you will find promises of God's presence right next to them:

> *The Lord is near.* Do not be anxious about anything, but in
> everything, by prayer and petition, with thanksgiving, present
> your requests to God. And the peace of God, which transcends all
> understanding, will guard your hearts and your minds in Christ
> Jesus. (Philippians 4:5–7, italics mine)

If you ever have doubts about this great promise, remember that Jesus is God in the flesh who has come close. His mission was, in part, to give his Spirit to us (Acts 2), and his Spirit is his presence.

> I will ask the Father, and he will give you another Counselor
> to be with you forever—the Spirit of truth. The world cannot
> accept him, because it neither sees him nor knows him. But you
> know him, for he lives with you and will be in you. I will not
> leave you as orphans; I will come to you. (John 14:16–18)

⇨ The Sovereign God is telling you that he *is* with you now and *will be* with you in the future. Do you believe this? Why or why not?

⇨ Does this truth compete with past experiences in your life when you felt abandoned? How do you square what God says with what you felt?

⇨ Has there been a time in your life when your confidence in his presence was a comfort to you? Describe it.

There are different ways to be present with someone. One way is to be physically present but passive and powerless. For example, a ship is sinking, and your friend stays with you. That can be a comfort, but the ship is still sinking and your friend can do nothing about it. God is not passive in his nearness. When God says he is present, it means he is doing something on your behalf. He is giving you manna. He is keeping promises and giving grace when you need it. God is never passive, and certainly he is never powerless.

⇨ What worries and fears do you have now? What difference will it make if you remember that God promises not to leave you alone?

"I *PROMISE* I WILL BE WITH YOU"

Sometimes a promise isn't enough. Imagine this scenario:

"The computer is for sale for five hundred dollars."

"Fine, I'll take it. I'll take the computer home today and bring you a check sometime next week."

Such a promise might work with a good friend, but if you don't know the person and don't have an address or phone number, you want something more than the person's word before you let him walk off with the computer.

A handshake? That is good for friends but not strangers.

"I promise"? That's no stronger than a handshake, not these days.

"I swear on the Bible," witnessed by a third party? That's better but not enough.

For something foolproof you must get his driver's license, major credit card, full credit report, and a legal contract that stipulates you will get his house and fifty-thousand-dollar BMW turned over to you if the check isn't in your hand by noon Wednesday. Plus, the BMW is in your driveway as evidence of the person's intent to make good on his promise.

Then you can sleep soundly. You can be fairly certain that the person's word is good.

That is what God does with his promise.

Human kings don't make promises. Elected officials make promises, but kings don't. A king might promise not to kill you if you swear to be his servant forever, but it is the lesser who makes the promises to the greater. When you are in the more desperate position, you are the one who makes promises. Remember the story of how Esau sold his birthright to his brother Jacob for a dish of stew? When Esau came in from the fields looking for dinner, he was in the more vulnerable position. He was starving; Jacob had food. So Esau was the one who made promises to Jacob. (For the full story, see Genesis 25:29–34.)

God, however, delights in making promises to you. Unsolicited, he makes one after another. This, of course, is his holiness on display. No mere human being will do such a thing.

But he is only getting started.

Next, he repeats the promise of his presence over and over. By doing this, God is both patiently reminding you and actually strengthening his promise.

Whereas you might underscore the certainty of a promise by saying, "I *really* promise," the Hebrew style is to repeat it, as in holy, holy, holy. So whenever you find the Lord saying, "I will be with you," realize he's said it many times and allow it to have a cumulative affect on your soul.

As if that isn't enough, your God then adopts the legal procedures of the day as a way to make you sleep easier. Without you asking, he brings out the lawyers, writes up a contract, swears to fulfill his promises, and shows it to you whenever you get anxious. In biblical language, these contracts are called covenants.

Abraham is an early example of someone with whom God entered into a covenant. It started with a promise:

> The LORD had said to Abram, "Leave your country, your people
> and your father's household and go to the land I will show you.
> I will make you into a great nation
> and I will bless you;
> I will make your name great,
> and you will be a blessing.
> I will bless those who bless you,
> and whoever curses you I will curse;
> and all peoples on earth
> will be blessed through you." (Genesis 12:1–3)

This is the grandfather of all promises. God had said to Abraham that he will take him—one ordinary person—and bless him with so many descendants that he will be the father of a great nation. Out of that nation will come the Messiah who, in turn, will bless the world and create a nation of faith that will cross all ethnic boundaries. In other words, the Lord will be with Abraham and never leave him or his descendants.

But time goes on and Abraham still has no offspring. He and his wife had become too old to have children. He is worried. Will the promise be fulfilled?

Here is what we think God would say if he were like us: "Abraham, I already told you what I am going to do. How dare you not believe me!" But God doesn't answer that way. Instead, he brings out the contract (covenant) with Abraham. The stars in the heavens become the guarantee:

The word of the LORD came to Abram in a vision:
"Do not be afraid, Abram.

> I am your shield,
>
> your very great reward."

But Abram said, "O Sovereign LORD, what can you give me since I remain childless and the one who will inherit my estate is Eliezer of Damascus?" And Abram said, "You have given me no children; so a servant in my household will be my heir."

Then the word of the LORD came to him: "This man will not be your heir, but a son coming from your own body will be your heir." He took him outside and said, "Look up at the heavens and count the stars—if indeed you can count them." Then he said to him, "So shall your offspring be."

Abram believed the LORD, and he credited it to him as righteousness. (Genesis 15:1–6)

A little later in the same conversation, God makes another promise to Abraham and confirms it with an even more binding covenant:

He also said to him, "I am the LORD, who brought you out of Ur of the Chaldeans to give you this land to take possession of it."

But Abram said, "O Sovereign LORD, how can I know that I will gain possession of it?"

So the LORD said to him, "Bring me a heifer, a goat and a ram, each three years old, along with a dove and a young pigeon."

Abram brought all these to him, cut them in two and arranged the halves opposite each other; the birds, however, he did not cut in half. Then birds of prey came down on the carcasses, but Abram drove them away.

As the sun was setting, Abram fell into a deep sleep, and a thick and dreadful darkness came over him. . . .

When the sun had set and darkness had fallen, a smoking firepot with a blazing torch appeared and passed between the pieces. On that day the LORD made a covenant with Abram.

(Genesis 15:7–12, 17–18)

In the contractual form of the day, God is swearing to Abraham that he will keep his word. The smoking pot symbolizes how God himself would accept dire consequences if the contract was broken. And it wasn't long before it is, indeed, broken. Abraham's descendants reject the Lord and follow other gods. But God had sworn to make good on his promise, which he does when Jesus pays the penalty for such insurrection.

⇨ What are you learning about the character of God?

⇨ Do you have hope yet? Are you beginning to think that your fears are actually opportunities to know God better, to trust him, and to witness how he will give you grace when you need it? Explain.

You already know you have received the updated and better version of the covenant. "'The time is coming,' declares the LORD, 'when I will make a new covenant'" (Jeremiah 31:31), and he has made it. "After the supper [Jesus] took the cup, saying, 'This cup is the new covenant in my blood, which is poured out for you'" (Luke 22:20).

> Christ is the mediator of a new covenant, that those who are
> called may receive the promised eternal inheritance—now that
> he has died as a ransom to set them free from the sins committed
> under the first covenant. (Hebrews 9:15)

The new covenant God has made with you is better than the one God made with Abraham. God will forgive and not remember sins (Jeremiah 31:34), the contract is eternal rather than temporary, and it includes the inheritance of the entire kingdom of heaven. These unparalleled blessings are just *some* of the results of the death and resurrection of Jesus Christ. "For no matter how many promises God has made, they are 'Yes' in Christ" (2 Corinthians 1:20).

⇨Do you understand why the Cross was necessary to secure the better covenant? How would you explain it?

⇨ How will you pray now that you are more certain of God's promises? Write out a prayer based on God's promise to never leave you nor forsake you.

Week 6 Goals:

- To know that fear craves a person, and that is exactly what you are given

- To be amazed that God would make any promises at all

- To be amazed that he will never leave you

- To be amazed that, when you have doubts, he responds by persuading you with even stronger ways of saying his promises

Week 7

The Lord Reigns— Things Are Not the Way They Seem

You have located fear, listened to it, identified how it can attach itself to money, death, and people, and you are learning that there is manna for tomorrow because the Lord promises he will be with you. As a final word of comfort, consider a psalm that can become your own.

A loved one didn't call. A trusted friend didn't show for coffee. Your mind races toward horrible scenarios. A horrible accident must have happened, and that person's life must be hanging in the balance. The bleak images become even more vivid.

Then the person arrives. Your loved one had run into some traffic. She had tried to call, but you forgot to turn your cell phone on.

Things are not always the way they seem.

The king of Aram has the prophet Elisha surrounded. It is strange that he'd sent out such a large war party to capture only one man, but he had learned that one doesn't take chances when one wants to capture prophets.

Elisha seems unperturbed by it all.

Elisha's servant, however, doesn't quite have his master's confidence in God. So when he sees that the two of them are surrounded by Aram's army, and knowing that servants typically receive the same fate as their masters, he is beside himself. If you identify with anyone in the story, you probably identify with the servant.

But the God of kept promises is faithful. The Lord reigns. Things are not always the way they seem. With the unaided eye, circumstances might indeed seem dire, but eyes of faith see that God is our strength and shield.

> When the servant of the man of God got up and went out early the next morning, an army with horses and chariots had surrounded the city. "Oh, my lord, what shall we do?" the servant asked.
>
> "Don't be afraid," the prophet answered. "Those who are with us are more than those who are with them."
>
> And Elisha prayed, "O Lord, open his eyes so he may see." Then the Lord opened the servant's eyes, and he looked and saw the hills full of horses and chariots of fire all around Elisha.
>
> As the enemy came down toward him, Elisha prayed to the Lord, "Strike these people with blindness." So he struck them with blindness, as Elisha had asked. (2 Kings 6:15–18)

As with the other stories in the Bible, this story is God's word to *you*. It is to encourage your confidence in the trustworthy God.

⇨ If your eyes were open, what do you think you would see?

PSALM 46

The writer of Psalm 46 certainly has his eyes open. He is persuaded that the God who made promises is faithful.

Consider making this psalm your own:

> God is our refuge and strength,
>> an ever-present help in trouble.
> Therefore we will not fear, though the earth give way
>> and the mountains fall into the heart of the sea,
> though its waters roar and foam
>> and the mountains quake with their surging.   *Selah*
> There is a river whose streams make glad the city of God,
>> the holy place where the Most High dwells.
> God is within her, she will not fall;
>> God will help her at break of day.
> Nations are in uproar, kingdoms fall;
>> he lifts his voice, the earth melts.
> The LORD Almighty is with us;
>> the God of Jacob is our fortress.   *Selah*
> Come and see the works of the LORD,
>> the desolations he has brought on the earth.
> He makes wars cease to the ends of the earth;
>> he breaks the bow and shatters the spear,
>> he burns the shields with fire.
> "Be still, and know that I am God;
>> I will be exalted among the nations,
>> I will be exalted in the earth."
> The LORD Almighty is with us;
>> the God of Jacob is our fortress.   *Selah*
> (Psalm 46)

The psalm divides into three stanzas, each one ending with "Selah."

First Stanza

In the first stanza the psalmist remembers that God helps when he is needed. Of course, you need him every day, but there are times that are particularly dire. Especially at those times he is an "ever-present help."

The psalmist is certainly in one of those situations. Things could not be more dreadful. He contemplates nothing less than the fragmentation of creation itself. The psalmist is envisioning an un-creation. The sea is breaking out of its boundaries and threatening another cataclysmic flood:

> God is our refuge and strength,
> > an ever-present help in trouble.
> Therefore we will not fear, though the earth give way
> > and the mountains fall into the heart of the sea,
> though its waters roar and foam
> > and the mountains quake with their surging.   *Selah*
> (vv. 1–3)

Second Stanza

The psalmist then shifts his attention from the chaos around him to the kingdom of heaven, where God reigns and his will is done. He is thinking about Jerusalem and the Temple worship. Wherever God is present, there is no reason to be afraid. The psalmist envisions the city. He is with God and God's people. What more could he want?

> There is a river whose streams make glad the city of God,
> > the holy place where the Most High dwells.
> God is within her, she will not fall;
> > God will help her at break of day.
> Nations are in uproar, kingdoms fall;
> > he lifts his voice, the earth melts.
> The LORD Almighty is with us;
> > the God of Jacob is our fortress.   *Selah*
> (vv. 4–7)

Some people try to use positive thinking to alleviate their fears. Instead, the Lord opens eyes to reality. He reminds that things are not the way they seem. When you are in God's kingdom—in the presence of the King—things are always proven to be better than they had seemed.

This stanza leads you to a familiar place: "The LORD Almighty is with us; the God of Jacob is our fortress" (v. 7). When in doubt, remember that promise. Since you will hear it again before the psalmist is done, it would be a refrain worth memorizing.

"The LORD Almighty is with us; the God of Jacob is our fortress."

This is unwavering confidence in God's promises, and the psalmist asks you to join him in that confidence.

Third Stanza

The final stanza of Psalm 46 points to the coming judgment day, and the psalmist looks to it with great joy. On that day God's justice will cover the earth. All oppression will be stopped in its tracks. Wars will cease, and both the injustices that start wars and the injustices that prolong them will be banished. Everything will be made right. *That* is a reason for joy and hope.

> Come and see the works of the LORD,
>   the desolations he has brought on the earth.
> He makes wars cease to the ends of the earth;
>   he breaks the bow and shatters the spear,
>   he burns the shields with fire.
> "Be still, and know that I am God;
> I will be exalted among the nations,
> I will be exalted in the earth."
> The LORD Almighty is with us;
>   the God of Jacob is our fortress.   *Selah*
> (vv. 8–11)

Notice that it is God himself who is speaking here. With a word, God will call all oppressors to attention. When he speaks they will immediately stop their wicked ways. The true King had been patient with the nations up to that point

79

by giving them time to lay down their arms and submit to King Jesus. Once he says "Be still," all rebellion against the King will cease. Everything will indeed end well.

You might notice a familiar voice in God's command to be still.

> That day when evening came, [Jesus] said to his disciples, "Let us go over to the other side." Leaving the crowd behind, they took him along, just as he was, in the boat. There were also other boats with him. A furious squall came up, and the waves broke over the boat, so that it was nearly swamped. Jesus was in the stern, sleeping on a cushion. The disciples woke him and said to him, "Teacher, don't you care if we drown?"
>
> He got up, rebuked the wind and said to the waves, "Quiet! Be still!" Then the wind died down and it was completely calm.
>
> He said to his disciples, "Why are you so afraid? Do you still have no faith?"
>
> They were terrified and asked each other, "Who is this? Even the wind and the waves obey him!" (Mark 4:35–41)

Jesus is committed to a thorough re-creation. What he does with the winds and the sea is a signpost that pointed to how he will reign and bring justice to all nations. This event with his disciples announces that the deepest sense of Psalm 46 is being fulfilled.

⇨ How does Psalm 46 and its fulfillment in Jesus encourage your confidence in God and give you hope? What are your initial reflections?

TODAY

With the Cross of Jesus proclaiming that your sins have been paid for, and with his resurrection assuring you that he is now the reigning King, you can trust him for the future and focus on today.

It is so deceptively simple: focus on today. Turn away from a worrisome future and face today with all its troubles and kingdom opportunities. This is certainly one application of Psalm 46.

Pray

Since today is filled with its own troubles, today starts with prayer—that's what you just did with the psalm. You know the King hears you, and you also know that prayer is the human vehicle that causes the kingdom of heaven to break through earthly strongholds.

The apostle Paul wrote: "The Lord is near. Do not be anxious about anything, but in everything, by prayer and petition, with thanksgiving, present your requests to God" (Philippians 4:5–6). This means that you should speak to the King about your worries.

Here is a way to picture what you are doing when you pray: you are coming before the King. You come with humility because he is, after all, the King, and you have nothing to offer him. He receives no particular benefit by having you as his subject. Indeed, you are costly to him. Even so, he invites you to come to him with your burdens, and he invites you to cast those burdens down. At first you assume that his servants will carry them away, but the King actually comes close to you and takes the burdens onto himself.

It doesn't seem right that your King and Father should take your worries on himself, but there is no reason to feel guilty for inequity in this relationship. Your King has always been the pursuer who loves you first, and he always will be. All you have to do is respond by praising him and telling others about his greatness.

> Humble yourselves, therefore, under God's mighty hand, that
> he may lift you up in due time, casting all your anxiety on him
> because he cares for you. (1 Peter 5:6–7, personal translation)

⇨ What is the connection between humility and casting your cares on God?

Get Busy

Prayer is the first way you focus on today rather than tomorrow. Then, after you have humbled yourself before God by casting your cares on him, you get up and get busy. There is a lot to do in the kingdom.

Let's say you have just failed at something important, or at least you are persuaded you have failed. You made a costly error on your job, you have spoken in public and looked inept, or your children were out of control in public. You feel miserable. The problem is in the past more than the future, so God's words to the fearful and anxious don't seem to fit.

But they do. Though the episode is in the past, you are still worried about the opinion of others. What are people saying about you now? What will they say about you when you see them again? Might you lose your job and the security that goes with it?

It is difficult to break old habits. You can still drift into the future and make predictions about how these things in the past might affect you later.

After you regain your spiritual footing and remember that the kingdom is about God rather than your own success, you fix your thoughts on today. That could mean that you get advice from someone about your children, or you give your full attention to the job your employer has given you.

When you direct your attention to today, your tasks are usually pretty mundane. You do your homework, clean the house, feed the kids, ask forgiveness of someone you have wronged, or prepare for tomorrow's houseguests. When Jesus entered human history and went about the normal tasks of life, he added gravitas to the ordinary. Now, when you do the chores that are right in front of you, you are following in the footsteps of the King.

And what are your chores? Your chores are to work and to love.

You can ask yourself these two questions: "As God's worker or servant, what job has he given me?" and "As God's ambassador of love, whom should I move toward in love?" Can you apply those questions to some of the following situations?

- A woman who lives in fear of another panic attack
- A man who rarely attends church because he fears open spaces
- A child who is afraid of germs and catching a disease
- A teen who feels self-conscious in almost any social situation

⇨ When anxiety strikes, what could you do "today" as you trust your Father for tomorrow?

In that rare case when you focus your attention on today and you still don't know what to do, a backup plan is available: you ask God and other people for wisdom. "If any of you lacks wisdom, he should ask God, who gives generously to all without finding fault, and it will be given to him" (James 1:5).

WHEN I AM AFRAID

When you pray for wisdom you might receive it right then, on the spot, straight from God. More often, though, God directs you toward other people. All you have to do is call a wise friend or pastor. If that person doesn't have suggestions, call someone else. You can be certain that, when you turn your attention to today, you will receive wisdom to know what to do.

Simple yet profound, isn't it? When you have hope for tomorrow, you can focus wholeheartedly on today. And God gives enough grace for today.

⇨ We always want to end by speaking to the Lord. How will you pray? You can practice casting your worries on your King and Father, who is pleased to receive them. But let's add one other thing. Pray for others too. Especially, pray prayers of blessing. In God's presence there is blessing. As he has said words of blessing that have comforted you, you in turn can speak words of blessing to others. Write out a prayer that includes blessing others.

Peace and hope be with you in Jesus Christ.

Week 7 Goals . . . and for Years to Come:

- To take delight in fighting fears because when you trust the Lord for tomorrow it honors him

- To talk to others about these wonderful mysteries that have been fully revealed

- To never doubt that God's communication to you in the Bible can speak to the deepest places of your heart

Final Thoughts

We hear lots of sermons, read good books, gather wisdom from friends, and read the Bible. We certainly don't lack for spiritual information. Because we are always dangerously close to overload, we can benefit by reflecting on the *one* thing that is important from what we have just read.

What does the Spirit impress on your heart? What does God say about fear and anxiety that is especially important for you right now? . . . Perhaps one of these:

- Anxieties as prophecies
- Manna
- My stubborn mixed allegiances and tendency to entrust my security to me
- The grace that will come when I see Jesus face-to-face
- Give more love than I try to receive from others
- The amazing character of the Lord and his promises
- How peace—Psalm 46 peace—can be a way to honor the Lord

For me personally? At this point I will pray that I will be a person of hope. Hope, after all, is the opposite of fear. Fear predicts the worst; hope says that my Father is working all things together for good and that I can trust him. This means I want to live with my eyes wide open and see how the kingdom of heaven is on the move, and it is aiming for the day when Jesus will return.

And you?